The Book of Random Language Facts

Sneaky Press

SNEAKY PRESS

©Copyright 2022
Pauline Malkoun

The right of Pauline Malkoun to be identified as author of this work has been asserted by them in accordance with Copyright, Designs and Patents Act 1988.

All Rights Reserved.

No reproduction, copy or transmission of this publication may be made without written permission.
No paragraph of this publication may be reproduced, copied or transmitted save with the written permission of the publisher, or in accordance with the provisions of the Copyright Act 1956 (as amended).

Any person who commits any unauthorized act in relation to this publication may be liable to criminal prosecution and civil claims for damages.

A catalogue record for this work is available from the National Library of Australia.

ISBN 9781922641205

Sneaky Press is the imprint of Sneaky Universe.
www.sneakyuniverse.com
First published in 2022

Sneaky Press
Melbourne, Australia.

Contents

Random Facts about Language   p.6

Weird and Wonderful Words   p.12

Random Facts about Language Families   p.18

Random Facts about Punctuation   p.28

Language Idioms   p.30

Idioms from other Languages   p.34

Language Jokes   p.36

Tongue Twisters   p.38

Random Facts about Language

The language with the greatest number of native speakers is Mandarin Chinese.

The language spoken by the greatest number of non-native speakers is English.

The language spoken by the greatest number of speakers is English.

Language is constantly changing.

It is thought that the most difficult language to learn is Basque, a language spoken in north-western Spain and south-western France. It has an exceptionally complicated vocabulary and grammar system and does not appear to be related to any other language in the world.

The country with the most languages spoken is Papua New Guinea which has 820 living languages.

Languages have existed since about 100,000 BCE.

At the time of print in 2021 there are 7139 languages spoken around the world.

The official language of a country is the language in which a government conducts business.

There is only one African country where the entire population speaks the same language, Somalia. They all speak Somali.

South Africa has 11 official languages.

Many languages in Africa include a "click" sound that is pronounced at the same time as other sounds. Languages which include "click" sounds must be learnt during childhood to achieve fluency.

More than 1,000 distinct languages are spoken on the African continent.

The Bible is the most translated book.

The first language ever written is Sumerian in about 3200 BCE.

The oldest written languages still in existence are Chinese or Greek from about 1500 BCE.

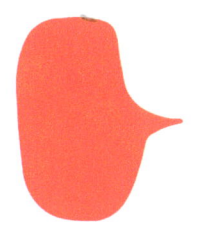

The most translated document is the Universal Declaration Of Human Rights, written by the United Nations in 1948, has been translated into 321 languages and dialects.

The most common consonant sounds in the world's languages are /p/, /t/, /k/, /m/, and /n/.

Half the worlds population speak one of the 10 largest languages in the world as their first language.

For 600 years, French was the official language of England.

Writing in Chinese does not include any punctuation.

The hardest tongue twister is thought to be: "The sixth sick sheik's sixth sheep's sick."

All pilots identify themselves in English on international flights.

The language with the most words is English, with approximately 250,000 distinct words.

The most widely published language is English.

The Language with the fewest words is Taki Taki (also called Sranan) with just 340 words. Taki Taki is an English-based Creole. It is spoken by 120,000 people in the South American country of Suriname.

The letters R, S, T, L, N and E are the most commonly used in English.

Weird and Wonderful Words

"Therein" contains seven letters, but with these letters, 10 words that can be formed using the letters consecutively: the, there, I, he, in, rein, her, here, ere, herein.

The only English word that has three consecutive double letters is "Bookkeeper".

The longest word in English that does not contain letter "e" is "Floccinaucinihilipilification."

It refers to the act of estimating that something is of little value.

Lung disease, "pneumonoultramicroscopicsilicovolcanoconiosis," is often considered the longest word in English. It has 45 letters.

"Unprosperousness", is the longest word in English where each letter is used at least twice.

The shortest word in English that has the letters a, b, c, d, e, and f is "Feedback".

Medieval music term "Euouae," is the longest word in English that contains only vowels. It's also the word with the most consecutive vowels.

The longest name of a country whose letters are alternating vowels and consonants is "United Arab Emirates".

The only word in English with one vowel repeated five times is invisibility.

The only feminine form of a word that is shorter than its male equivalent is widow.

The 5 most commonly used words in English are: the, be, to, of, & and.

The word "set" has the most definitions in English.

The capital of South Korea, "Seoul" means "the capital" in Korean.

"Queue" is the only word in English where even when the last four letters are removed, is still pronounced the same.

In English, nothing rhymes with month, orange, silver or purple.

The only eight letter word in English with just one vowel is "strength".

The only number where the spelling is in reverse alphabetical order is "one".

The only number who's spelling matches the number it represents is "four".

The only number where the spelling is in alphabetical order is "forty".

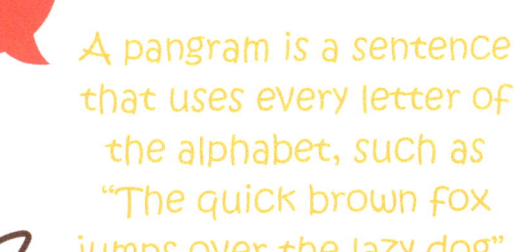 A pangram is a sentence that uses every letter of the alphabet, such as "The quick brown fox jumps over the lazy dog".

The longest word in English without a vowel is "Rhythms".

"Screeched," is the longest one-syllable word in English.

Random Facts about Language Families

Languages are classified into families based on similarities because of a common language ancestor from which they evolved.

The Indo-European language family is broken up into smaller families which include languages spoken in India, Pakistan, Iran, and nearly all of Europe.

Similarities between the ancient Indian language, Sanskrit, Latin, and Greek were noted in the early 18th century.

The Indo-Iranian family includes languages such as Urdu, Hindi, Bengali, and Punjabi, spoken in Northern India and Pakistan. Persian and Kurdish are also a part of the Indo-Iranian language group.

The Romance language group developed from Latin. It includes languages such as Spanish, Portuguese, French, Italian, and Romanian among others.

The Germanic language group includes the Scandinavian languages (Swedish, Danish, Norwegian, Icelandic, and Faroese) as well as English, German, Dutch, Flemish (which is spoken in a part of Belgium), and Afrikaans (which is related to Dutch and is spoken in South Africa).

The Slavic language group includes Russian, Belarusian, Ukrainian, Polish, Czech, Slovakian, Bulgarian, Serbian, Croatian.

The Greek language group includes modern and older forms of Greek.

The Celtic language group includes Breton, Irish Gaelic, Welsh, and Scottish Gaelic.

The Baltic language group includes by Latvian and Lithuanian.

The Finno-Ugric language group includes Finnish, Estonian, Saami, and Hungarian.

Basque as far as we know, has no known language relatives.

The Turkic language group, includes Turkish, Azerbaijani, Uzbek and Kazakh.

The Afro-Asian language family is found in the northern and eastern parts of Africa. This family is usually divided into five sub-groups with the Semitic group of languages the most common. This is the family of Arabic, Hebrew, Amharic and Tigrinya, as well as the long extinct Egyptian language, which is known for its hieroglyphics.

The Niger-Congo language family is usually divided into ten sub-groups with each sub-group including several hundred languages.

The Khoisan language family is spoken in southern Africa. These languages include the click sounds.

The Nilo-Saharan language family includes all the other languages spoken in Africa.

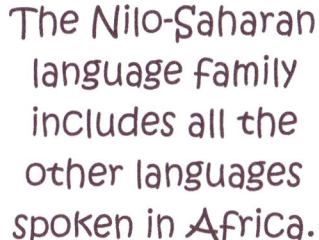

It includes the Nilo language group which consists of about 150 languages spoken by people in east Africa. The Saharan language group includes 10 languages spoken in Chad, Niger, and Libya.

The largest family of the Niger-Congo is the Bantu language family. These languages are spoken in Sub-Saharan Africa and include Swahili.

The Malayo-Polynesian language family includes languages spoken in Asia and Oceania. It includes languages such as Javanese, Indonesian, Tagalog (found in the Philippines), and Malay which belong to the Western branch of the Malayo-Polynesian language family.

The Eastern branch includes the languages of the Micronesian, Polynesian, and Melanesian communities including the languages spoken in Fiji and the Maori language of New Zealand.

The Dravidian language family is spoken southern India and includes Tamil and Telugu.

The Australian language family includes the 250+ indigenous languages spoken by the First Nations people of Australia. These include Walpiri, Arrernte, Kuwarra and Nyangumarda.

The Sino-Tibetan language includes the languages of China, such as Mandarin Hakka, Wu, and Yue (Cantonese) and Burma, Tibet and Taiwan, however the relationships between the languages of this family are unclear and disputed.

Like Basque, both Japanese and Korean do not have any known language relatives.

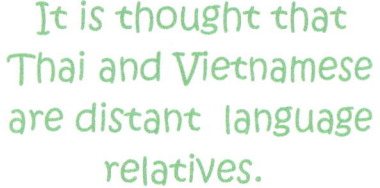

It is thought that Thai and Vietnamese are distant language relatives.

The relationship between the approximate 700 languages spoken on Papua New Guinea (the Papuan language group) is unknown. They have been grouped into a family because of the geographic proximity.

The American Indian language family comprises of about 20 language families with a few languages in each of the indigenous peoples of the Americas. This family includes Quechua which is spoken in Bolivia and Peru and Guaraní which is spoken in Paraguay.

Random Facts about Punctuation

The @ sign has a range of (funny) names. In the Netherlands, it is called the "monkey's tail", in Israel it is called a "strudel", in Russian it is the "little dog", the "small snail" in Italian, and the "crazy A" in Bosnian.

is actually called an octothorpe because it has eight points.

The exclamation mark didn't get its own dedicated typewriter key until the 1970's.

The "full stop" has been around since the 3rd century BCE and it used to be placed at the top of a line rather than at the bottom.

It is thought that the comma and the full stop were invented by the same man —Aristophanes of Byzantium— to show actors how individual passages of text should be read.

Ampersand used to be a letter 27th letter of the English Alphabet (it meant 'and').

Early writing did not have any punctuation (or spaces).

Language Idioms

If you are at a loss for words, you don't know what to say.

To eat one's words is to admit to being wrong about something you said earlier.

If something is beyond words, are no words that can describe it.

To go back on one's word means to break a promise.

To have had words with someone means to have argued with them.

To have a word with someone is to have a short conversation with them.

If something goes without saying, it is so obvious it does not need to be said.

If something is all Greek to you it means you do not understand what has been said.

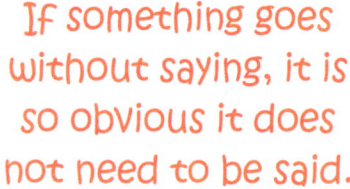

If two people are speaking the same language, they agree and understand one another.

If someone is talking in circles, they keep repeating the same points.

Talk is cheap means it is easier to say you will do something than to actually do it.

When words fail someone, they can't find the words to express their shock or surprise.

Idioms in Other Languages

Portuguese

Ter macaquinhos na cabeçachuva.

Literal translation: You have little monkeys inside your head.

What it means: To have a crazy idea.

Spanish

Se me fu eel avion.

Literal translation: The airplane got away from me.

What it means: I forgot.

French

Les Carottes sont cuites.

Literal translation: The carrots are cooked.

What it means: The situation can't be changed.

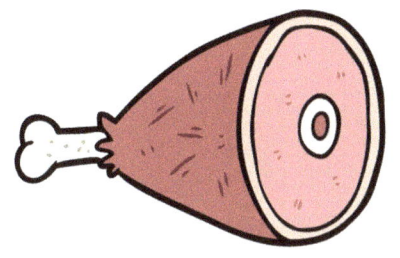

Italian

Avere gli occho foderati di prosciutto.

Literal translation: To have one's eyes lined with ham.

What it means: Cant's see something directly in front of you.

Russian

Говорят, что кур доят

Literal translation: They say they milk chickens.

What it means: Don't believe everything you hear.

Arabic

القرد في عين أمه غزال

Literal translation: In his mum's eyes, the monkey is a gazelle.

What it means: Love makes even the ugliest people seem beautiful.

Language Jokes

I'm close friends with 25 letters of the alphabet; I don't know Y

I was walking past a farm and a sign said: "Duck, Eggs" I thought: That's an unnecessary comma - and then it hit me."

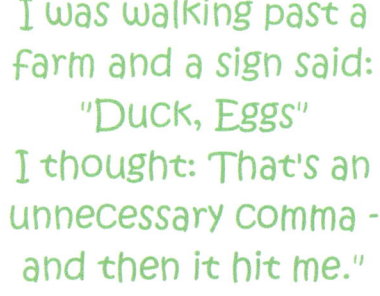

What do you call Santa's little helpers?

Subordinate clauses

Which dinosaur knows a lot of synonyms?

A thesaurus

What language do stomachs speak?

Hungarian

Knock knock!
Who's there?
To
To who?
Actually, it is to whom?

Why did words, phrases and punctuation end up in court?

To be sentenced.

Why did Shakespeare only write in Pen?

Pencils confused him, 2b or not 2B.

The past, present and future walked into a bar.

It was tense.

Tongue Twisters

If a dog chews shoes, whose shoes does he choose?

Peter Piper picked a peck of pickled peppers.

How much wood would a woodchuck chuck if a woodchuck could chuck wood?

I have got a date at a quarter to eight; I'll see you at the gate, so don't be late.

She sells seashells by the seashore.

I thought I thought of thinking of thanking you.

He threw three free throws.

Wayne went to Wales to watch walruses.

A skunk sat on a stump and thunk the stump stunk, but the stump thunk the skunk stunk.

Four fine fresh fish for you.

Other titles in the Random Facts Series

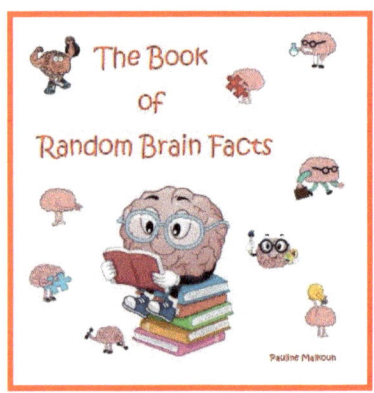

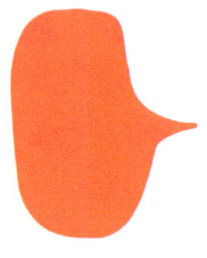

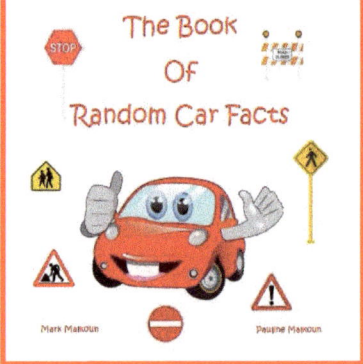

www.ingramcontent.com/pod-product-compliance
Lightning Source LLC
Chambersburg PA
CBHW051249110526
44588CB00025B/2928